The Moon is a Pill

Aušra Kaziliūnaitė

About the translator

Rimas Uzgiris is a poet, translator, editor and critic. His work has appeared in *Barrow Street, AGNI, Atlanta Review, Iowa Review, Quiddity, Hudson Review, Vilnius Review* and other journals, and he is translation editor and primary translator of *How the Earth Carries Us: New Lithuanian Poets*. Uzgiris holds a Ph.D. in philosophy from the University of Wisconsin-Madison, and an MFA in creative writing from Rutgers-Newark University. Recipient of a Fulbright Scholar Grant, a National Endowment for the Arts Literature Translation Fellowship, and the Poetry Spring 2016 Award for translations of Lithuanian poetry into other languages, he teaches translation at Vilnius University.

The Moon is a Pill

Aušra Kaziliūnaitė

Translated from Lithuanian by Rimas Uzgiris

The translation of this book was supported by the
Lithuanian Culture Institute

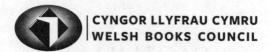

Parthian, Cardigan SA43 1ED
www.parthianbooks.com
First published in 2018
© Aušra Kaziliūnaitė 2018
© Translation Rimas Uzgiris 2018
ISBN 9781912109456
Design and layout by Alison Evans
Printed by Pulsio

contents

part four

part five

part one

holy

pedestrian smiles, a cold spring, books, films
shoes in the wrong spot, sex, monday's sirens
a pigeon flies into church—
none of it appears to mean anything

and that's the only reason
it appears

stuffed

one day, by the dumpster, i saw an abandoned stuffed bird
i saw it and forgot, but it didn't forget me, it even began to
    stalk me—
wherever and whenever i would go, whomever i would
    meet, i saw the ragged bird

at first, i pretended not to see it
let it show itself, what do i care – it neither chirps nor pecks
    at me

but eventually, it grew rude – appearing not only in public
    places—
among students, listeners, pedestrians—
but showing up among friends, perching even on my loved
    ones' heads

so i tried to make nice, asking – what are you doing here
    and what do you want?
but the stuffed thing just squatted there – silent
and my father, on whose head it eventually perched, only
    looked at me enquiringly
dad – i whispered – there's a bird on your head!
but he just waved his hand, you know – big deal

from that time on, i began to see the stuffed creature in my
    dreams—
no escape – i hardly slept, i barely ate, i barely was—
and i would keep seeing it – always frozen in the same pose,
    mute, frayed,
though it began to seem to me that it was smiling – the
    stuffed bird was mocking me

so i finally snatched it up and threw it with all my strength
  at the wall, only, it turned out,
that wasn't the wall, but a mirror.

that was the first time i saw a bird fly
in a mirror

the blooming bush

i don't remember much of childhood—
often getting sick, i had nightmares, i feared the dark
i had no friends, sometimes, i was afraid of vanishing,
of just disintegrating like a cloud—
there's almost nothing more
and when i try to remember
it seems that i always had a fever
that when i broke my leg, i had to learn to walk again

another thing – my mother got especially angry once
and broke off a branch of this yellow blooming bush in spring
and i didn't care at all
but pretended to cry

after that, i went to school, finished school, had boyfriends
and girlfriends, matriculated in a BA programme, graduated
matriculated in an MA programme, graduated, matriculated in
  a PhD programme
and always tried to be very excited about all of this
because i was trying to the last to hide from myself the fact
that it didn't really matter to me

and now, slowly, i begin to understand
that this dripping from the tap
the dead cats lolling on my lap
the fog slinking over the land
all of the words of the people i once met
and all of the yellow blooming bushes of spring

recognised me

before i was born

4

minotaur vacations

in the landscape, calmly
a woman drowns

from the lifeguard
stand echoes

attention!
a woman drowns in the landscape

suddenly
you fall and cut yourself
on god

and slivers of clouds
calmly swim in the sky
as if nothing
had happened

as if
giant beavers
did not gnaw
at the tree of the world,
or minotaurs wander
in our veins
or
the fish of sadness
did not intend to drink
everything,
small worthless fish

whose river
reflects
slivers of clouds
drowning above us

whose landscape
reflects a naked woman—

you could scoop out
with a teaspoon
or by the handful
her eye
nose
breast
or shoulder

and the woman would feel
nothing

a birdless night

is just a lake
where two nude
mermaids fondle
their white marble bodies
and night
pours over the bank

i sit on a well-made
bed
dangling my feet
and catch the sound
outside my window
of the rustle of
branch-ripened
morning

one frightened mermaid
slaps her tail in retreat,
a few drops of night
splatter my walls

i sit and stare
at how she dives
deeper and deeper
into herself

as if she would want
to mine the cove of dreams

and day breaks

ice-fishing

you sit
at the bus stop—
pedestrians
hurry by,
traffic flows

a giant hook
hangs in the air
baited
with everything that ever was

one by one
the cars bite down—

colossal drops of blood
dribble from their jaws
and
fall on
golden groves
where the blackest night
lies in wait
where trees
touched by the wind
make music
without a single curse—

then

they flutter and gasp—
like this morning
that has swallowed
you

omelette

i was planning to cook an omelette
i broke one egg
then another
and in the third i found a grimy boy

sitting there, parentless, alone
in a shopping mall
with a small box at his side

i looked around to see if anyone saw
then continued to prepare
breakfast

plants

i arranged myself
on the shelves
of grocery stores

poured myself into the gas tanks of buses
where it's dark and tight
but at least there's a direction – maybe a meaning

i wrote my name at bus stops
but nobody gets on there

i checked myself out
of all the municipal libraries
and forgot to return myself

i feel the weather changing
i feel the debt growing

and that spring is coming
spring is coming
spring is coming

with me

spring dissection

a lone man walks the park's paths
he strides with ease
dissecting the body of spring
wanting to know why, and forgetting what for

veined hands, sunken cheeks
sometimes he knows what he wants, especially today

the metal he grips in his pocket is still cold
his shoes are made of finely worked leather
there is some cash and a few cards in his wallet
on one of them, he is smiling today

he walks on the lawn trimmed for the first time this year
the scent is so strong that even his tobacco-dulled nose can
   smell it
he wants to figure out the reason why spring dies
maybe even write a novel

he bends down and drives a knife into the ground with all
   his might

the cuts, drawing blood, are almost perfectly straight
he sticks his hand inside and searches, and searches
until he pulls out a small blue car
the same one that he once lost as a child

spring that's love

and you're standing there, vanishing in sunlight
buried under an avalanche of spring
lost for all time

there is nothing else but light
and more light
you try to pry your eyes open
to see what there is to see
and capture it
while feeling the vanity of that endeavour

warmth caresses your face, the blinding sun
a refreshing river of wind purls over your skin
and you need nothing else

how can you need
when you have at your finger tips
the light of all the suns that have ever sparked
and on your lap
the delicacy of all the flowers that have ever faded

all flowers wilt

i hear a knock, i open the door:
my neighbour from the other side of the wall

i used to hear her, in the evenings, washing up
i've seen her out of the corner of my eye a few times—
the first time was in childhood
when our dog Lord didn't come home
and again
when grandmother didn't come

i always tried to do what was intimate quietly – so she
    wouldn't hear
in truth, the most ordinary things became intimate because
    of her

holding my breath, my heart quivering, at one in the morning
i would slowly and quietly stir honey into my camomile tea
so that she wouldn't hear, so that she wouldn't understand

and here she is standing in front of me with a giant, red
    bouquet of blossoms

their heads bob with satisfaction in my trembling hands

stunned, like some fool, i ask

what should i do with them?

she smiles so beautifully, beautifully

just love them

invisible metamorphoses

would you love me
if suddenly my gender
changed or my scent
the colour of my skin
the time of year

would you still love
if i were a flower and a stone
or a flower growing
among stones

and
generally
do you love me

in those blinks of an eye
when i am truly
there

part two

part two

the moon is a pill

the moon is a pill
with a groove
down the middle

anger is a pill
with a groove
down the middle

Mindaugas Bridge is a pill
with a groove
down the middle

summer is a pill
with a groove
down the middle

drought in Africa
that wipes away
the lives of five hundred thousand children
is a pill
with a groove
down the middle

a beloved woman is a pill
with a groove
down the middle

a cop striking the protestors' dog
is a pill
with a groove
down the middle

to give up one's seat on the bus
is a pill
with a groove
down the middle

to sing from joy
having buried one's self
is a pill
with a groove
down the middle

silence is a pill
with a groove
down the middle

drunken time lies
in the groove
and babbles

never ask
who cut this groove
who dug this day for us
who nailed a twitching bird
to its teeth
BREAK IT

swallow one half
and the other—
opening the bird's lid with both hands
insert the pill and close

then you will finally
see—

drops of blood
streaking
over the day's teeth

if i lose my hands while walking
don't pick them up and don't
run up to me to give them back
they were simply too heavy
they were too heavy
and that's that

you can take them home
to decorate a Christmas tree
homeless cats won't touch them
they were too heavy
just too heavy

if i lose my head while walking
don't say
you're so unlike yourself today
so not like yourself—
there were creatures inside, creatures
who were hunting me

if i lose my words while walking
don't pick them up from the soggy ground
let them lie there in the dirt
they'll sprout when spring arrives

the meadow will rustle where teenagers gingerly touch

if i lose the rain while walking
go outside
it's me, it's me
caressing you, without hands

no, thank you!

you're walking the narrow streets of the medina-quarter
you turn the corner
and there's no one there, no vendors, no pedestrians
just charcoal shadows and soured pigeon shit

eventually, at one corner after another, you find volunteers
    to show you the way
they follow you, insinuating that if you run from them you'll
    lose your way

a small boy runs by your side, mocking you: no, thank you!
    no, thank you!

and then – a square, a tree, a person
wrapped in cloth, he could be one of Jesus's friends

'so go, go, and don't stop, and don't listen to what they say
you're like those donkeys who go without stopping, go until
    they die'

and i go on, i go listening to how the old man under the tree
    rages
i turn in circles, always meeting those who want to show me
    the way
thinking, maybe i really need to stop, let them lead me astray,
    rob me

maybe when you're led astray you're less lost than when you
    lose yourself

fortune

in a flash, i am all those people for whom fortune smiled
but they are afraid to smile back
so they look down at their feet and blush

they just look down and blush

even though no one has smiled for some time

in a flash, i am all those people who feel superior to others
and all those people who feel inferior to others
and i am
a snail
a live snail in a North African bazaar

i find myself
in a coiled basket with other snails

slowly unfurling my antennae

tourists pass
taking pictures

you have to live somehow

every night i hear the herons leaving
every morning i see the falling leaves
every day winter comes somewhere
without end
every evening i am buried by a man
wearing denim overalls

he doesn't earn enough for this
but you have to live somehow
pay your mortgage
child support too

he grins

rain in Vilnius

gravediggers
dig out the city little by little
lower us into it nailing it up
then scatter rain on top

at first—
by the handful
later—
with shovels

later yet—
they cover us with silence

holiday make-up

i saw angels with automatic rifles in their hands
staring sadly at the floor in airports and stations

waiting

i saw eight-year-olds sent by their parents
running up to human rights activists
shouting – give us back the rainbow—

giggling

i saw men who thought they were real men
and women who thought they were real women
saying in greeting, instead of a name—
i am so and so's woman—

i saw emptied villages, forests felled
dammed rivers and steeples of small towns

in the mirror

part three

part three

alien planet

the computer says – we've arrived
it's generally not very talkative, but has been jabbering
for hours now about the pruning of fruit trees
it says – we have reached our journey's goal

my toes are numb
i climb out of the spaceship
and look around, gathering samples for scientists—
i walk about a room identical to my own
nothing lives for light years all around
there are no curtains
it's quietly snowing outside
garlands glitter in windows across the street
children push and shove on the sidewalk

nothing but cosmic loneliness and stone

signal lights

lying in the heads of dream people
in the entrails of forgetting and remembering
thoroughly digested and digesting
you suddenly turn over to the other side
so that you could wake up
in the already dreamt dreams of dream people
and when the town executioner cuts off the head of dawn
you arm yourself with the sharpened blades of unease

you skip along like a summer breeze
like freedom that knows no will
like a desert jackal scenting the carrion of victory
separating you from the executioner's neck

another split-second
AND

it's cold,
a red light
blinks in the distance—
an alarm sounds
in the neighbouring house's lot

lifting your eyes
you see the entire sky
is full of similar lights and unease—
stars that don't blink, but burn

that
is the alarm
sounding above
from a long time ago

a longer time than we have been
a longer time than the word has been
proclaiming that someone
is stealing—
that someone stole the sky

and so what, if god is a seagull

all our history of trying to see, craves not to see

for so long we looked for confirmation
that this time it's for good, that now everything is really real
that to the very grave, etc., etc.

time and time again, we wanted clear and tangible evidence
something concrete and visible
but so what if it's there, and so what if god exists

and so what, if god is a seagull, turning his head to all sides
    in disdain
swallowing fishes live, and shitting on a Belarusian writer

and so what if god is orange juice
whose expiration date is missing and which
some uncle Stan bought for breakfast some six years ago

and so what, if god is that athletic young man
with brown eyes, showing the exact measure of his penis
on a gay website

and so what, if god is—
only we don't notice him

as in the sky, so in

i see clouds

looking at dragons, knights and castles
i see only clouds

i see one cloud domesticated
with a whip and
a town

the sky of the town—
an unmade bed

and the seagulls of town
still remember us—
the unprayerful

but their squawks recede
on the wind usurped
by pitiless
red tenement tracts

bloody red-ement tracts
that spit out a black-haired maid
who makes the bed

of clouds i see
swimming by
amazed at her dexterity

as she removes the seagulls
and changes them
for something fresh

idyll

i'm sitting on the bed
and hear the birds outside the window
i smell potatoes frying
and see myself among them
in the uncertainty of fortuitous lumps

this one has my grinning lips
rolling greasy on the ground

so i say to myself:
now everything is really all right
now everything will finally be real

the bed, birds, window and potatoes
all assent:
now everything will finally be real

second storey

from my windows i can see
the trolley bus wires
take people away

electricity sparks and
dies

pupils narrow
and expand

blood flows to my temples

and a buck restlessly raises
his head

to listen for the unheard murmur
of the night he just imbibed

when the city empties us

no, i'm not drunk
i'm empty

the city is drunk
it has emptied us
it filled us too

now it dances
and sings
it smokes and laughs out loud
invites us home
and stands on all fours

when the city empties us
we find a place for ourselves
and can enter into our own selves
to walk about in the dark

and hear how the embers crackle
but not see
how they go out

a city in a city

a city flows
everyday
from a shampoo bottle
onto your hair

at the place where
you get a ticket
for parking
the full moon
in the wrong
spot

someone is cutting
a clearing
for a camp
in a tenement
apartment

they build
the day into it
and walk
arm in arm
down the street

storm

on your body – tattooed rain
falling leaves splashing
cars in the old town
and i—

my wet tattooed
clothes, torn shoes
and soaked hair

but there is no
umbrella
here

and no
you
on your body

an old woman walking a fighting dog

i saw them
slowly slipping
along the sidewalk
snorting into
winter's bowl

they struggled forward
so differently

that they became
the only thing
that wasn't a curse

wardrobe

i saw another person's dream
trying you on for size

it washed and ironed you
hung you in the closet
then threw you away—
you were just too big

occasionally i meet
the homeless man
who wears you now

finally, there is light in his eyes

coltsfoot will grow along the fence

someday, all my friends will die
my relatives and loved ones too
my enemies will die and all my neighbours
the passers-by whom i once met on the street
will vanish from the surface of the earth

my classmates and colleagues
teachers professors co-workers
will die

all the people will breathe their last
with whom i wore
for reasons unknown
the same uniform of time
though i never fought
in any of its battles

birds who once flew
above my head held high
will die and the dogs i used to hear howl
on spine-chilling nights outside the city
will grow silent for all eternity

coltsfoot will still grow along the fence
tired grapes will rest on arbours
but no one will call me by name
and i myself will not be

but then
carefully
head slightly cocked
i'll watch the strange dogs
grapes and coltsfoot

and then
for the first time
i'll really see the flight of birds

and the couple hurrying by
will scroll
their eyes
along the bench
on which i sit

and they will know
that i see
the flight of birds
differently

and that
i am
those things i don't know
the dogs the grapes
and the coltsfoot

part four

part four

from the memoirs of a sad god

i cut a person out of the river

i took the first stencil into my mitts
that came walking down the street—
the shadow that was created
before the one who cast it

and i cut and i cut
and i sawed—

a round head
two arms of similar length
two legs of similar length

i cut a person out of the river

he flows in waves
sputters and
doesn't move

but
you won't step twice
into him

the evening news

i'm watching this person—
he's been walking
the supermarket aisles
for two hours now

i come up to him and say,
good day—
he shakes his head
and continues searching

he finds a shelf

it's stacked with packs
of toilet paper
most often four
closely packed together
you see – that's how
they reproduce

the man comes up to me
and says,
toilet paper—
i shake my head
and begin to see

golden fleece, fur, an apple and us

Run, comrade, the old world is behind you!

we walk out the backs of churches
we look for a fitting street
in which to drink the leftover night
we look for a fitting street
in which to scream out our leftover light
we are broken mufflers, yes,
we are ashtrays
trams
and tears – up until that moment
when you give them a reason to be

we rot away on the inside
and the waiter on Île St. Louis
drives us from the outdoor café
he's dressed as a hippie
a huge peace sign, purchased
for one euro, hanging around his neck
he touches my hand, counting to three:
it's that kind of party, you know

i can hear the breaking bones of cars
and my laughter, your laughter
no, no, not that laughter
the other one, the one you don't know
until it happens that
the mufflers all fall off
and the lights go out
and ashtrays are emptied by a gust of wind
Vulcan melts them down in his hearth
of laughter, the other laughter
winking, he gives you a thumbs up—

like a Persian cat
that bona fide
factory of hair
the production manager, director-in-chief
repeatedly licking himself in public
with no shame or other bullshit
then choking on his own products
spitting out a hair ball

that's us
searching for a street in which to disavow ourselves
because the public toilets are all full

we search for a long time, finally
something heavenly happens
finally
we clear our throats and cough out
a lump of light

let it go to the nursery
let it climb a tree
let it play in the sandbox
with dogshit and other goods
in other words, let it live

or

drive on up to the sky
and give the sun
some time off

horse races

at the camp, people's bodies lie about on horse manure
unmoving, but running
snoring

and they don't die

if they were dead, we would say
how cruel, there were little kids there
they cried for a few minutes after they were shot
and it would be very very sad, and we would look at
    each other
meaningfully, then go to Maxima to buy white bread and
we would watch TV shows, doing everything to forget
    more quickly
we would rearrange our furniture, talk about art
copy out a recipe for cake from a book, talk about art again

but now that they're not dead, lying in the camp, in the pen,
    enclosed
and surrounded by soldiers, stretched out on racehorse dung
we hate them more than ourselves, and we do everything to
    forget them
as quickly as possible
we go to Maxima to buy white bread, we watch TV shows

we go to Maxima to buy white bread

with trembling voice

i fantasised about something that has to happen
about the Vilnius Cathedral and the Vilnius Christmas Tree
about Vilnius' little children gathered
to listen to stories in the room inside the Tree

i fantasised a secret agent, a girl with trembling voice
coming to read stories about Vilnius' princesses and princes
and Vilnius' gnomes
to Vilnius' children

instead of stories, she takes out a blood-stained book by
    Lautréamont
the same one who inspired the surrealists, the one who wrote
about girls with twisted hands, about girls eating their
    own hands
about boys next to whom you sit in parks
'when you become the ruler of others, you'll be able
to do them as much good as you once did evil'
about a person who sews up his victim's eyes and pretends to be
her saviour, serving her, not out of repentance,
but just for fun

and the Vilnius girl would read in the Vilnius tree to Vilnius
    children
not about Vilnius princesses, Vilnius princes and Vilnius gnomes
but about edible brains and practical satanism

because you have to fight evil with good

freedom

an old writer looks at me with disgust
and squeezes some words out through his teeth:
who can stop you from writing what you want?
we must understand that his times were those of censorship
and we now live in a greenhouse like some kind of tomatoes

who can stop you from writing what you want?
asks the fish with bulging eyes in the unseen stream of time
who can stop you from writing what you want?
wonder aloud Mickey Mouse and Mr. Jesus
holding hands in the orifice of dreams
in which i drown did drown and will drown

who can stop you from writing what you want?
ask the clams and seashells the waves gulls and seaweed
the drowned ship's captains and the innocent maidens—
in a decade they'll give toasts as they drink each other's blood
by the monument to Anderson's mermaid or some other hotel

who can stop you from writing what you want?
uneasily stammers the glass in the windows of block apartments
with clouds drifting by

i turn to them all and say—
you can all stop me and so can
the red in a cluster of rowan berries

the rug of time

we're like the fish
in the bathroom
rug

nattering
gasping
all fluffy
and mild

avoiding
the question:
whose bathroom is it?

gallery

we sit and someone plays boom
boom in the other room someone
drinks wine chats kisses

i go deeper into the forest
wading through the dewy carpet
overgrown with greenery
my bare feet caress moss
and i pick a berry
maybe a gooseberry

made up of little beads
made up of playing sitting
chatting heads

who don't see
the moon rising
now
over the hill

i will be your man

i will be your man
i will be your wife and children
i will be soft furniture
and pictures on the wall
i will be silence and no touching

you will see yourself in my eyes
and you will ask

why does winter come at times
why do my hands sometimes shake
and what do the trees do
left all alone
in the forest

part five

part five

i haven't read a poem

i haven't read a poem in a long time:
surrounded by the impassable bogs
of philosophy, the impenetrable
forests of novels in translation—

i dreamed a creature there

not a serious beast
sort of yellow
brooding

maybe a jay

only a hundred-page jay
but already a beast

i haven't read a poem in a long time
because it doesn't fit
into three hundred pages
the jay doesn't fit
either

it takes more time
it takes all time

i haven't read a poem in a long time
because it doesn't fit
because it takes

i haven't read this poem

on autumn love without commas

a person
is a river
on which ducks
swim with empty
plastic bottles

and the one and
the other are equally
beautiful to you

so you could stand
like that for hours
overtime
on the bridge

in autumn's jar

in the city's autumn streets and squares
you can catch the scent
of death cooking

and your heart is filled
with maddening joy
you want to run and scream
and swing your arms about

but you sit on a bench
paging through a book
waiting for the trolley bus
then you go to the store

holding a secret close

while death in autumn
opens her kitchen
windows just a crack

and you feel, finally
in fact,
alive

a thousand and one deaths

a man swallowed
the bridge
from which the sun
had once jumped
and then received
its disability compensation

now,
in its belly
sits saturday—

the saturday
full of years
when
we folded herons
out of the starry
sky

when our work
was done
they had nowhere left
to fly

20% concentration camp

night grows
outside the window
one and the same
while the days are many

and those, separated
by years,
write each other
into the family tree
and have no inkling
of how graceful
the fall will be

when we sit on a terrace
overgrown
with clusters of moonlight
and drink the terrace down

when on another day
utterly alone
walking through an old garden
you'll hear a horrible roar

or when beyond the gates
you see
a speeding emergency
vehicle

you will think
how many more people
die here
than there—

on the other side of the fence

hope

i don't do the work i like to do
i avoid the people whom i love
i don't talk to those whose presence i enjoy

only by doing dull things and
hanging out with shitty people
can i believe that the world is beautiful

the apocalypse or a toothpaste commercial containing some characteristics of the apocalypse

And power was given unto them over the fourth part of the earth,
to kill with sword, and with hunger, and with death,
and with the beasts of the earth.
Revelation 6:8

to tear with the teeth of the beasts of the earth
to repeat with the teeth of the beasts of the earth
to be stupefied and to say goodbye
with the teeth of the beasts of the earth
to press the crosswalk button
with the teeth of the beasts of the earth
to cognise and recognise
with the teeth of the beasts of the earth
to ask without waiting for an answer
with the teeth of the beasts of the earth

as if a traveller tossed
from his shoulders
a raw leather bag
and from that bag
night's ocean poured

as if it had
the teeth of the beasts of the earth
with the teeth of the beasts of the earth

the hamster running in the sun wheel is himself the sun

every morning the sun rises
and every morning it sets

over and over again
an old Spanish translator
hangs out in the dark
corridor

talking about Saramago
with whom he says he spoke
the very day he received the Nobel prize
and
Gabriela Mistral
he says – writes about women, very hot

he criticises my eating habits
and never asks me anything
except – why do you smoke?
but he waits for no reply

he says
he knows all
the truly important writers
so when i come to Madrid
he'll definitely introduce me—
maybe soon the whole world will know you,
it's not impossible, ha ha

he translated Latvian poets
but claims they are nothing compared to the Spanish
his judgement of writers is determined by the number of
languages that translate them—
without translators they would be nothing

he says—
it's good to be a translator
it's very very good to be a translator

his eyes sparkle, he smacks his lips
and adds, with a dreamy smile—
but it's bad to be a writer, very bad,
you will have to find a way to handle your enemies, ha ha

but sometime
long ago
he was in love, truly,
and his head was once clear and pure,
made from thin glass
almost like a transparent vase
designed to hold water
for the most beautiful wildflower bouquets

a fable about a castle, a rat (maybe dead), petroleum and Stalin

someday
we'll live at home
and feast on stars
we'll eat all the stars
or at least those
dusted with sugar
we'll take down the constellations
while talking about love
or truth
and there won't be
anything left to shine at night

and there won't be any war
and there won't be any terror

white rivers will flow
for five days straight
we'll give them to each other as gifts
and drink to each other
remembering mother's milk

someday
we'll live at home
and there won't be any war
and there won't be any terror

and there won't be
any us
because we
are fish
king size
fish
who have eaten their home

seasons

✖✖✖

even when nothing else is left
the crumpled sheets remain
the deep breaths
and your fingers
on the body of summer's end

autumn
trees drop
the cawing of crows
into all
our mirrors

ice
one more careless step
one more stupid smile
and the ice splits, cracking
now i'm really falling
into you

spring
sitting next to you i can smell
the wounds under your clothes

magnolia blossoms
pushing through your skin

✖✖✖

wildflowers
at city cafés
steeped in soda bottles

that's us

zero's eclipse

the crosswalk sign
has pierced
a person

but it doesn't hurt
since silence too
needs
spring

morning is drawn slowly
from the atom
on the left—
cigarettes
coffee
birds

and the leeches of time
cover us—
passers-by
hurrying
anywhere—
leaving behind
large dreams

because—

hey, full moon
there's a button
undone on your face

button it, already
please

Acknowledgements

The publisher would like to acknowledge the publications in which these translations have previously appeared:

Druskininkai Poetry Fall Anthology, Gobshite Quarterly, How the Earth Carries Us: New Lithuanian Poets, Lituanus, New Baltic Poetry, Vilnius Review.

Parthian Baltic Poetry

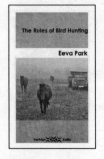

The Rules of Bird Hunting

Eeva Park

Phenomena

Eduards Aivars

Beasts

Krišjānis Zeļģis

Narcoses

Madara Gruntmane

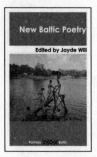

New Baltic Poetry

Edited by Jayde Will

Now I Understand

Marius Burokas

PARTHIAN

www.parthianbooks.com